KU-540-974

{ *Collecting for Tomorrow* }

Candlesticks

This series is written by experts and specially designed for the collector who is interested in modestly priced and readily available items of the 19th and 20th centuries.

Other titles available in the series:

Kitchenware by Jo Marshall
Spoons by Michael Snodin and Gail Belden
Boxes by Brian Cole

Collecting for Tomorrow

Candlesticks

Deborah Stratton

Pitman Publishing

10 AUG 1976

HERTFORDSHIRE
LIBRARY SERVICE

749.63. 7509630

First published in Great Britain in 1976
by Pitman Publishing Ltd
39 Parker Street, London WC2B 5PB

© Walter Parrish International Limited 1976

All rights reserved. No part of this publication may be reproduced, stored in a retrieval system, or transmitted in any form or by any means, electronic, mechanical, photocopying, recording or otherwise, without the prior permission of the copyright owner.

Designed and produced by
Walter Parrish International Ltd., London

Made and printed in Great Britain by
Purnell and Sons Limited,
Paulton near Bristol, Avon, England

ISBN 0 273 00234 1
G48:14

To Norman and Sara

Contents

Author's acknowledgements

I gratefully acknowledge the help given to me by Laila Iversen of Troll Antiques, Susan Benjamin of Halcyon Days and Michael Snodin, in the collecting of information for this book.

Introduction

The candlestick that we take so much for granted today as an attractive decorative addition to the dining-table was for centuries the main method of lighting in homes and places of work, as well as in public and sacred buildings. For us, candlelight means cosy French restaurants, romantic dinners, relaxation—beauty glittering on a stem of glass or silver. But until the 19th century, when lighting by paraffin lamps became customary, life depended on the wax or tallow candle and its holder.

Oil lamps and candles as a means of lighting had not changed much even up to the Middle Ages. There were candle 'pendants' or beams of wood, with iron or brass pans for the candle, and wrought-iron implements to hold rush lights or candles. Pewter holders were a sign of wealth. All the early sticks had a pricket—a simple, skewer-like fitting in the centre of the pan—and the candle was pushed down onto the skewer which held it upright.

Brass or bronze candlesticks were pre-eminent from the 14th to the 17th century, silver and gold being reserved for royalty or the church. The socket, or nozzle, reached Europe from Persia some time during the 14th century, and by the end of this period it had superseded the pricket almost entirely, except for some very large floor-standing church sticks which are still made today, particularly in Spain and Italy. However, the simple rush holder continued in use in small homes and rural areas until well into the 1700s.

Very few early silver sticks survive from before 1600 except in church treasuries. About this time increasing prosperity in Europe and a sudden flood of metal from the mines of the New World established silver as the favourite in elegant households. Brass became the poor relation, and the brass foundries, instead of setting new fashions, were reduced to copying silver forms.

As the 18th century advanced, the simply moulded Queen Anne styles flourished, particularly in the American colonies where they remained popular until the 1880s. But highly ornamented rococo designs alive with foliage, swirls and asymmetrical scrolls took over, at least in silver and the new porcelain. Then the classical revival swept everything before it—silver, porcelain, brass were shaped into columns, festooned with garlands and acanthus leaves. The neo-classical style reached America a little later and, since it coincided with the new government, is known as the Federal period.

English lead glass was developed around 1675 and by the 1770s there were glass sticks of every description from tiny single taper-sticks for the desk to huge chandeliers, strung with crystal beads and drops, holding twenty or thirty candles. Some glass followed silver styles, in particular Queen Anne mouldings, but the vogue for cut-glass decoration started, and still continues today. In general, the simpler the cutting, the earlier the date.

With the Victorian era, the development of oil and the electric light, candlesticks took off into wildly decorative shapes which still continue. Every possible shape and style was tried out, beribboned or festooned, flowered or plain.

American glass of this period led the world in sheer invention, and candlesticks followed every season and whim, from the charm and simplicity of early pressed glass, the ingenious coloured and cut extravagance of art glass, the end of the century, the revolution of Art Nouveau and Tiffany, the huge amount of Frederick Carder, depression glass of the thirties, right up to the 'Scandinavian' influence of clear crystal and heavy polished forms still popular today.

For the collector, candlesticks have seldom been treated as a separate subject, being generally described and sold according to their material; wooden and brass sticks in particular usually in furniture sales, the others as objects of silver, glass, pottery, etc. But all sticks have a unique aspect—they must above all reflect their function. They must be stably constructed with sturdy bases, securely fastened sockets, light enough to carry; in short, few categories display so well the eternal equation—function plus design equals beauty,

Practical advice to a collector is simple; learn about styles and materials generally so you can judge the age—few sticks except for silver and porcelain were marked. There are almost no books on candlesticks alone, so look for information on general subjects such as furniture, decoration, silver, glass, Art Deco, etc. As a beginner, never be ashamed of buying broken or damaged examples (which should be very cheap indeed) to learn about construction and patina, but for your collection try to avoid cracks or severe chipping. If you do buy one because the subject or type is rare, then the price should be less than you would pay for a perfect piece. As far as price is concerned, it is impossible to even begin to suggest the actual cost of any candlestick. What might be expensive today is ridiculously cheap tomorrow, and fairly costly the day after.

There are antiques and collectors' magazines which specialise in giving up-to-the-minute reports on dealers and auction prices. Visit the dealers, go to the auctions and see what brings the best prices. Remember that condition is very important—particularly with 20th-century stems since, generally speaking, they were mass-produced and there are plenty of perfect examples around. This becomes less important with earlier examples.

Occasionally, a collector may find a pre-18th-century stick at a reasonable price, but, practically, the collecting period covered in the book spans the last 200 years, with particular emphasis on the time since *c.* 1880.

Any stick should be well balanced so that it holds the weight of the candle easily. Glass nozzles were sometimes cracked and replaced. If you are offered an old metal stick, it should show normal signs of wear, particularly on the base and inside the nozzle. Learn the difference between well made, smoothly polished brass of even twenty or thirty years ago and cheap modern copies from Birmingham or the East knocked up as tourist souvenirs. On the other hand, remember that souvenir sticks are a comparatively untouched field, and could make an amusing group.

Those who collect candlesticks will find that for an outlay of a few dollars or a pound there are single items that complement a collection, that can be used and which may in future become members of fields that command large followings and possibly large prices. Pairs, as a general rule, are worth more than twice as much as a single stick. But, in my opinion, much of the fun of collecting comes from acquiring many singles, preferably of exceptional quality, cheaply.

Glossary

AIR TWIST: Technique used in glass stems to create spiral decorations. Originally English, 1750s–1770s, revived in England and America from the 1950s to the present day.

BALUSTER: Architectural term for the turned posts that support a rail. Refers to the stem of a candlestick which is shaped like a baluster.

CHINOISERIE: Western application of Chinese motifs and designs.

DRUM: Base of candleholders fashioned in the shape of drum.

FOOTRING: Rim attached to base of candlesticks or other objects to protect against damage.

GADROONS: Repeated curved shapes very common on metal as design motif on parts of candlesticks such as their bases and sockets.

KNOP: Swelling or knob, such as those on candlestick stems whose function was decorative and to catch candle drips.

NOZZLE: Candlestick socket into which the candle is placed.

QUATREFOIL: Four-leaf motif found in medieval or Gothic and Gothic-revival design.

SAVE-ALL: Device used in mid-17th century to allow candle to burn to the end without damaging holder.

SNUFFER: Implement for trimming candle wicks so that they burned efficiently, also for putting out the candle efficiently.

SWAG: Drooping garland of flowers, fruit or drapery used to ornament classical furniture, architecture, candlesticks, etc.

TENON: Projecting part of the candlestick stem inserted into the top of the base and flattened outwards in order to hold the two parts together.

TREFOIL: Ornamental three-leaf motif such as clover shape.

TURNER: Woodworker who turns wood into shapes by revolving it on a lathe and shaping it with cutting tools.

Iron and wooden candle-holders

The form and features of candlesticks are very much related to their function, and these functions are clearly reflected in the various types of iron holders. There are rushlight holders composed of simple long clips on a stand. There are coil and socket sticks and pricket sticks.

Before paraffin became the standard material, candles were made of wax or tallow. A wick formed from rush, cotton or flax was basted or dipped repeatedly into the melted material until of sufficient thickness to form a candle. Candles could also be made by heating a lump of wax, applying it to the wick and rolling it into shape. Wax, being harder (and incidentally more expensive), was better suited for pushing onto a spike or 'pricket'.

The simplest candle was a rushlight with a thin coating of fat. These rushlights and their holders were common in the poorer homes of the 17th and 18th centuries. Sometimes they incorporated socket-type holders for candles. The socket candlestick probably evolved to hold the weaker tallow candle and small candles. There were wall and table models, and floor holders, just as there are for modern electric lights.

Another common type of 17th- and 18th-century candle-holder was the coil steel spiral on a wooden base. This and the steel cage type operate on a 'lift' principle to bring the remains of the candle higher up in the holder as it burns down. They were used in cellars, barns and stables well into the 19th century.

Because of the inability of wood and iron to withstand rain, worm, and rough treatment, few early examples have survived. 19th-century examples are usually the oldest available to the collector. They are most often found in rural communities rather than urban shops, and forgotten on the walls of old farm buildings.

Remember to clean rusted iron carefully or it will flake into pieces; an oily rust remover is best. After wooden pieces are cleaned, they can be polished with wax to bring out the colour and protect the surface.

A special kind of early wooden candle-holder was made into an adjustable stand. The stand was either threaded like a screw so that the cross-arms holding the candles at either end could be moved up or down, or the light was moved by a ratchet device. On a third type, the cross-arms were held by wedges.

Iron and wooden candle-holders of types common in humble homes of the 17th and 18th centuries and in barns, stables and cellars of the 19th century, height 12 inches. Both the coil on the left and the cage on the right have primitive 'lifts' which move the candle up as it burns down.

Pottery

Pottery has had a long and rich history and it was often used for candlesticks that were intended for use rather than ornament. None-the-less, the humblest wares were often decorated in an attempt to make them pleasing.

The early red-wares were humble and basic, used in the kitchen, dairy and as tableware with wood and pewter. These were often decorated with charming trailed and sgraffito patterns, made by scratching through the glaze before firing to leave a white line motif.

Stonewares of varying fineness were also made in abundance, with some of them approaching the thinness of porcelain. They were harder than earthenwares and were glazed by having salt thrown over them during the firing process which created a rough, glassy coating. Usually grey, they were decorated with free-hand painting in cobalt blue or, less often, brown.

In America, some of the best known were Rockingham wares (yellow body with brown mottled or streaked glazes) and Bennington pottery.

A variety of creamwares were also made in America, but the most popular came from Josiah Wedgwood's English pottery. In fact, similar preferences were shown for other European ceramics and so the American pottery industry suffered for some time from competition from abroad. American stoneware production increased greatly after the Revolution and continued until the late 19th century.

Floral decoration on pottery and porcelain was very popular during the Victorian period and painting flowers on plain white china and coloured glass was a favourite pastime of ladies in England and America from the 1860s.

The earliest examples tend to show moss-rose, auriculas, pansies and lilies-of-the-valley. Later, cabbage roses, dahlias and peonies were popular. Still later, in the 1870s and 1880s when the vogue for Japanese design was at its height, peach blossom, ferns, rushes and sunflowers appeared frequently.

Candlesticks were made in all these wares, mostly small and simple, but always there was the urge to decorate and ornament.

These particular candlesticks show how hard it is to distinguish the unmarked wares made in England and America, particularly the simpler kinds. They do show that Victorian American women often preferred English pottery to show off their artistic talents.

Victorian Staffordshire pottery candlestick, height 5 inches, hand-painted by an American woman.

Creamware

Pottery lamps burning oil for light date back as far as Roman times if not further but pottery holders for candles were in use only from about the mid-17th century. Unfortunately, most have not survived although great quantities were undoubtedly made.

In the 18th century moulded white candlesticks of salt-glazed stoneware were charming products of Staffordshire in imitation of porcelain. But in terms of refinement and practicality, creamware was far better—a lightweight pottery with a smooth creamy glaze.

Creamware was soon made all over Europe and America; factories turned to creamware for simple useful objects that were usually moulded and then left undecorated to show off the glaze.

A number of English potteries produced candlesticks in the neo-classical style of a Corinthian column with its characteristic capital and vertical fluting. Leeds is one factory noted for the making of such candlesticks, from about 1780 throughout its history (including periods of operation under other names) until about 1878. Early examples are finely moulded with good detail in the swags, acanthus leaves and fluting. This pair has lost much of such detail but it makes an extremely inexpensive addition to a collection, reflecting the neo-classical style so important in all materials from the late 18th century onwards.

There was a particularly enthusiastic revival of this style among Victorians of the late 19th century, and of course there are modern interpretations even today.

Victorian creamware candlesticks, height $7\frac{1}{2}$ inches, made in the shape of Corinthian columns. The lack of detailed modelling indicates a late 19th-century date.

Blue-and-white earthenware

Blue-and-white earthenware was made in great abundance in England from about 1780 to 1850. With its variety of Chinese themes, English and American views and universally appealing colours, it is much collected on both sides of the Atlantic, and even early examples such as the one pictured here are not expensive.

European blue-and-white wares were inspired by the Chinese who had made blue-and-white ceramics with underglaze, blue-painted decoration since about 1300 A.D. Dutch Delftwares and English blue-and-white wares of the 17th century were early European imitations and from the early 18th century European porcelain manufacturers were even more successful at imitating Chinese blue-and-white.

But until the technique of transfer-printing decorations on ceramics was developed in the latter half of the 18th century, Chinese-style blue-and-white ceramics were not available to the majority of people. The method involved making a print from a copper engraving and transferring this to pottery in the biscuit state before applying the glaze; it was an early mass-production technique which allowed a large quantity of earthenwares to be decorated from each copper plate.

'Chinese' designs were always popular, but English scenes and other themes were soon introduced and these too were greatly sought after. North America was a huge export market, and many of the wares were decorated with American scenes and flourished about 15 years before the start of Queen Victoria's reign in 1837.

Most pre-Victorian examples are unmarked but an educated guess as to the factory of origin can be made by analysing glazes, foot-trims, and other physical characteristics, and comparing these with marked examples.

Thousands of different patterns were made and the same ones used by different potteries. Look for good rich colours and clean outlines and details in the pattern, and a clean smooth glaze. The pagodas, trees, Chinese figures and border decorations on the example illustrated are typical of the Chinoiserie designs on English and Welsh blue-and-white pottery and porcelain.

Although many blue-and-white pottery candlesticks and chambersticks have been produced in England in Staffordshire, Lancashire, Yorkshire and Northumberland and in South Wales, few have actually survived intact the regular use to which they were subjected. Most often, the bases and candle sockets are chipped—try to find undamaged pieces if you can.

Blue-and-white Staffordshire pottery chamberstick, width $5\frac{1}{2}$ inches, c. 1830, with Chinese-style scene printed under the glaze by the transfer-printing technique.

Wedgwood

The firm of Wedgwood established in 1759 produced candlesticks mainly in Queen's Ware and Jasper and a few in basalt. The first examples were copies of silver styles made in black basalt.

Wedgwood's reputation in the Midlands, indeed in the whole of England, gave him access to many sources of information and modelling talents. The firm's most famous modeller was John Flaxman who also designed items of silver. Celebrated for neo-classical designs, he was described as 'more classical than the Parthenon'.

A close friendship between Josiah Wedgwood I and Matthew Boulton, the Birmingham inventor, engineer, industrialist and silver-smith, resulted in exquisite pairs of candelabra or girandoles made of cut glass and Jasper drums, mounted in ormolu or silver.

Because of the immense affection of collectors, 18th-century Wedgwood candlesticks are rare and expensive. However, there are many 19th- and 20th-century examples on the market.

Over the years, the firm produced not only classical designs but a number of highly unusual models, including a figure of Triton embracing a whorled shell supporting a candle-holder. There is the 'Seasons' pair with tree trunks forming candle-holders; in one a Cupid holds a basket of fruit symbolizing summer, and in the other, presumably emblematic of winter, he stands by a fire.

Wedgwood's most popular candlesticks have been made of his outstanding creation, Jasper. It resists candle heat and smoke, and stains wash off easily. This 'white porcelain biscuit of exquisite beauty and delicacy' (his own words) was more suited to the classical revival than possibly any other single material. The non-porous body was 'washed' or dipped in blue, sea-green, black, crimson, turquoise, pale green, buff and other colour variations.

In the 1760s, Josiah Wedgwood developed a fine, elegant ear-thenware which had something of the durability and beauty of his more expensive products; the result was named Queen's Ware after his patroness, Queen Charlotte, and it revolutionized tableware by bringing the pleasure of owning Wedgwood within reach of most people.

Queen's Ware remains popular today, and even modern examples are worth collecting for the future, since they often reproduce classic designs.

Candlesticks in all colours and sizes, including American pressed-glass examples, have dolphin bases.

Wedgwood dolphin candlestick, height 9 inches, first produced in 1776. This is a modern reproduction in Queen's Ware from an original Josiah Wedgwood model. This form is also made in the fine-grained stoneware black basalt, developed by Josiah in 1769.

Dresden

Successors to the famous Meissen Factory were the 19th-century porcelain makers of Dresden, Vienna and other places throughout Germany. Their products are usually known collectively as 'Dresden'. Many candlesticks of ornate design, characteristically formed by the modelling of figures and foliage, were copies of 18th-century Meissen. Turquoise, pink and gilding were popular Dresden features, as were Cupids, birds and floral encrustations covering the whole of the item.

This tendency to over-elaboration prevailed in factories all over Europe, such as Sèvres in France and Derby in England. Other factories outside Germany also continued to imitate Meissen figure and foliage modelling. Thus Meissen, which in 1710 began production of hard-paste porcelain in imitation of the Chinese—and was the first successful factory to produce porcelain products for any length of time—had tremendous influence on porcelain throughout Europe.

The factory at Meissen, near Dresden, was noted for the fine quality of the porcelain paste, its palette of luscious enamel colours and the excellent sculptural modelling of figures, animals, flora, fruits, musical instruments, etc., executed by J. J. Kändler. When Meissen's designs were applied more and more during the 19th century to the making of decorative centre-pieces such as candlesticks and candelabra, the original Kändler moulds were translated into a profusion of blossoms and leaves, Cupids, birds and fruits. Bases once left plain to emphasize the finely modelled figures were usually also decorated and coloured. Nevertheless, the quality of modelling was still excellent and a collector will find much of interest among these imitations of Meissen originals at a price most can afford. Many are still made in Germany.

Because of the elaborate work and the damage that occurs over the years, modest collectors will be satisfied with one rather than a pair. Any damage greatly lowers the price, and therefore the appeal to the investor, though a flaw in the midst of a heavily decorated item may hardly alter the overall appeal to the collector.

Dresden porcelain candelabrum, height 8 inches, c. 1840, showing the elaborate details and the colours characteristic of the 19th-century successors to Meissen. The quality of the modelling of the female figure is technically superb if a little stilted.

Art Deco pottery

Art Deco is a term that has been almost universally adopted to cover all design in the decorative arts between World Wars I and II. It is therefore not one style but many. Yet in bringing together a number of recurring themes, colours and design motifs it has, in the sum of its parts, an easily recognizable character.

Art Deco, or 'Art Moderne' as it is also called, reflected the moods of the days of the 'bright young thing'. The influences on design were many. They included the new concept of speed in the form of the car, motorcycle and, above all, the aeroplane; bright and exotic colours as seen in the costumes and sets of the Ballet Russe when it performed in western Europe were also very influential.

The development and use of new materials such as plastics and chrome revolutionized everyday products. At the same time, new discoveries in archaeology created a strong craze for 'Egyptian' art, which was reflected in the Movie Palaces so typical of this period and the parallel curved lines emphasized on everything from windows to ashtrays.

Candlesticks provided an excellent means for showing the new shapes and colours and were very popular in all materials. They could also be used for current design motifs such as the stylized grapes shown in the photograph.

Ceramics and plastic were particularly suited for communicating the craving to be, above all, modern. Clarice Cliff, who designed for her husband's Newport Pottery and is now considered to be an archetypal designer of the period, called her brightly coloured patterns 'Bizarre' and 'Fantasque'—words that aptly describe much Art Deco.

A number of artist-designers worked for the Poole Pottery in the 1920s and 30s, producing highly decorative ceramics, hand-painted with stylized flowers and birds in delicate pastel colours. Many other firms, such as Doulton, also produced Art Deco pottery.

Right: Single pottery stick, height 11¾ inches, from the 'Bizarre' range designed for Newport Pottery by Clarice Cliff, leading designer of the late 1920s and the 30s. Centre: Poole Pottery candelabra, height 11 inches, and marked 'Poole England', a mark used by the firm after 1925. Left: One of a pair of Poole candlesticks with stylized grapes, height 7 inches, marked 'Poole of England'.

Pewter 1

Pewter candlesticks dating from earlier than about 1780 are scarce and expensive. However, a great many tall baluster-shaped sticks which are well worth having, in terms of quality, attractiveness and increasing scarcity, were made from about 1780 to 1860. All pewter made before the 20th century has a certain rarity value and is generally much loved by collectors for its mellow colour and rustic associations. But it was considered a humble substance for much of its history and became valued enough to preserve and cherish only towards the end of the 19th century, after a great deal of it had already been destroyed or melted down for re-making.

Pewter was made and used in Roman Britain in the 3rd and 4th centuries A.D. but there are few candlesticks in existence made prior to about 1660.

Between 1660 and 1710, a heyday for the pewterer's craft in terms of high quality and originality of design, candlesticks had octagonal bases and wide drip-trays along straight cylindrical stems with bands of reeding or rings. Later in the period came decorations consisting of grapes and vines on the bases and baluster stems with a variety of knops. Towards the end of the 17th century, with improvements in candle-making, drip trays disappeared.

Pewter candlesticks appear to have been largely supplanted by brass and pottery from about 1715 to 1760. Thereafter many were made with a huge number of variations to the shape and location of knops and tear-drop designs, and they had iron push-rods running through the centre to eject the candle stub.

Many of these styles continued to be made throughout the 19th century and are reproduced to this day. Countless fakes of 17th-century candlesticks and other early pewter have also appeared in this century, but the collector should learn quickly from colour and touch whether an object is new or old. Even fairly recent pewter will have acquired a patina, or sheen, that is very different from the mechanically polished shine of new metal. Some old pewter has 'touch' or 'bench' marks, but the large majority of pieces will not be marked at all.

Selection of pewter candlesticks. The tallest pair, c. 1800, are 13¼ inches high. The next pair in height (7¼ inches) are c. 1830, as are the tapersticks (4¼ inches) in the background. In the foreground are 18th-century tapersticks (height 3¾ inches). Tapers were very slender candles used for feeble lighting or for melting sealing wax.

Pewter 2

To find American pewter candlesticks made earlier than the 19th century is rare. The North American continent did not have its own tin mines and had to rely on tin, the main ingredient of pewter, from Cornwall in England. The English trade, anxious to protect its interests, imposed stiff duties on the tin, at the same time encouraging the colonies to import ready-made pewter products by making them duty-free.

Nevertheless, the American pewterers produced candlesticks and other items of superb quality in simple English styles: many of these have worn out and been re-fashioned into later styles; others have long since been snapped up by collectors who arrived early in this field.

Collectors of modest means will have to look to English and continental pewter candlesticks from the late 18th century and early 19th century and to American pewter from the 19th and 20th centuries. Many of these will be so-called 'Britannia Metal' candlesticks made by spinning sheets of metal into shape on a wheel, as opposed to the traditional method of casting. Britannia Metal was the name given in the late 18th century to a substance similar to pewter, but which was made almost entirely of tin and antimony, contained no lead, and could be spun. Modern pewter is virtually the same. Like plated silver, pressed glass and transfer printed ceramics, Britannia Metal offered the means to make more goods available to more people at lower prices. In America, Britannia Metal articles were made from about 1825. However, its introduction both in America and England also heralded pewter's decline, as other materials—glass, ceramics and silver—were preferred.

Lately, however, the pewter industry has undergone a revival in England and America and reproduction pewter candlesticks are increasingly in demand.

As early pewter is so scarce, many fakes appear; unless candlesticks are obviously of 19th- or 20th-century manufacture and hence not valuable enough to fake, it is much the wisest course to buy from a reputable and knowledgeable pewter specialist (except when the price of a proposed purchase is low enough to warrant taking a risk).

American mid-19th-century 'spun pewter' (Britannia Metal) candlesticks, height 6 inches, and bed-lamp or chamberstick, height 4 inches. The bed-lamp is of a traditional 18th-century design and the candlesticks hark back to the 16th century when the drip-pan began to move up the stem, eventually ending up under the socket or as the flange on the nozzle.

Art Nouveau pewter

Art Nouveau stood out from the mainstream of the late Victorian and Edwardian decorative arts, and was generally noted for high quality workmanship as well as artistic conception in design. A revival in hand-crafts, notably metal-work, resulted in a great many candlesticks that deserve pride of place in a collection. There are not only mass-produced items to be found but also individual craftsmen-made items that are still relatively inexpensive.

Art Nouveau is regaining popularity though the organic tendril shapes that creep through English examples and the thin, pallid, rather dead-looking females entwined in candlesticks, vases and lamps were out of favour for a long time.

'Tudric' pewter, the name for a range of ware put out by Liberty & Co. from about 1901 to the early 1930s was, like Liberty's 'Cymric' silverware, inspired by Celtic design. Archibald Knox (1864-1933) was responsible for many of the firm's designs, but designers were not identified on the products. Marks include 'English Pewter', 'Liberty & Co.' and 'Tudric Pewter'. Knox was more controlled and conservative in his designs than were many exponents of Art Nouveau.

Generally, the earlier candlesticks are better made and more original, the late ones becoming merely repetitive. One of the first and most successful designs in 'Tudric' was a stylized 'honesty' seed pod design of interlaced stems with seed pods inset with coloured enamels on copper. The firm of W. H. Haseler in Birmingham made most of Liberty's pewter and silver.

Liberty & Co. of London is an important name in Art Nouveau because it made available to a large public (at prices they could afford) fabrics, metal-work, furniture, glass, ceramics, jewellery and miscellaneous goods by some of the movement's top designers.

Candlesticks and chambersticks from the Art Nouveau 'Tudric' pewter range sold by Liberty & Co. around the turn of this century. The tallest stick in the background is 8 inches high. The plant forms typical of Art Nouveau are combined with shapes of Celtic inspiration. The hammer marks on the hand-beaten candlestick were popular with designers because they were obvious signs of hand-made work in the midst of so many uninspired mass-produced goods of the time.

Wood 1

Wooden candlesticks have been in use from earliest times; wood and rough pottery were probably the first materials to be used in the home. The wood may have been a base for iron rushlight- and candle-holders or a complete candlestick—because of its ready availability from nearby forests.

However, few examples have survived because of their relative unsuitability to the task of providing light by fire. When forgotten, the early quick-burning tallow candles must have often dissolved down to the flame and set the candlestick, and, sometimes, the entire house, alight.

In England carved wooden candlesticks were fashionable during the 18th century. A number of these which have the sensible feature of metal or metal-lined sockets have survived. As wood is hard to date, the collector must compare similar styles in hall-marked silver and look for signs of age, wear and polishing on the surfaces.

Apart from the elaborate and gilded candlesticks and candelabra, candlesticks of woods such as walnut, mahogany and lignum vitae were often made as beautiful examples of the turner's art.

Twist candlesticks—either solid as pictured here or open-twist—were specialities of turners, who developed their craft with the invention of the lathe around 1450. They have all been popular ever since, but the double and triple open twists require the greatest amount of skill. In older examples the wood was cut away from the sides but in more modern specimens the turners have removed the centre core from inside the spiral twists with a drill.

During the various antique revivals of the Victorian period, 17th- and 18th-century styles in wood were reproduced. The machine then took over much of the turner's job.

Countless Victorian and Edwardian wooden candlesticks based on antique styles were machine-turned. The oak barley-sugar twist pair shown here are late 19th century, but are of a type which continued to be popular in Edwardian times and in the 1920s and 30s.

Late Victorian wooden candlesticks based on antique styles. The tall oak pair of barley-sugar twist design, height 12½ inches, are a type reproduced in great numbers during revivals of the Jacobean style and later in the 1920s and 30s. The smaller pair, of ebony, a wood fashionable again in the late 19th century, height 7¾ inches, are a Georgian baluster-shape found in candlesticks of other materials.

Oak with brass inlay

The term 'Gothic Revival' (or Gothick) refers to a style which was influenced by the church architecture of the Middle Ages. It is often used to describe furniture and other artefacts, especially candlesticks since they lend themselves to the vertical lines sweeping high and heavenward which were characteristic of Gothic architecture.

Gothic forms have continued to influence design to this day, notably in church candlesticks. This pair of 20th-century German candlesticks, while not necessarily designed for an altar, have a Gothic feel in the upsweeping curves, combined with a cleanness of line associated with the Bauhaus group of artists and designers who were functioning in Germany at this time and who influenced modern design to such a great extent.

The Bauhaus movement was headed by Walter Gropius, and his work, together with that of Mies van der Rohe and Richard Newton, had an enormous effect on all the decorative arts. They and their students designed houses for themselves and large commercial buildings, supervising details such as fabrics, furniture and accessories.

The Gothic aspect is further emphasized in the trefoil designs drawn in inlaid brass. Gothic windows and tracery were often expressed in trefoil shapes. The brass itself can be taken as a modern substitute for gilding which was often carried out on Gothic decorations. The brass inlay used in conjunction with sturdy oak—along with the clean, modern lines of this design—helps to lend lightness and grace to these candlesticks which would otherwise look rather lifeless and dumpy.

German Gothic design was characterized by elaborate detail and a fondness for tracery work—traits repeated in the 20th-century examples shown here.

German oak candlesticks, c. 1920, height 8 inches, with elaborate trefoil clover-leaf brass inlay pattern. While displaying the clean lines of modern design, these candlesticks convey a neo-Gothic style associated with altar candlesticks, especially in the inlay which is suggestive of the tracery work in Gothic windows.

Wood 2

There is an honesty about wood that appeals to many collectors. It is a pure material that cannot be mixed with any other without this being readily detected. Most other materials used in the making of candlesticks—ceramics, glass, pewter and silver—are made up of various components which must be melted into liquid form before they can be fashioned into objects. Wood, whether carved by hand or turned on a machine, is the same material that grew from the ground.

Although wooden candlesticks can be splendid examples of the woodworker's art, they have never been a truly effective means of lighting. On a practical level, wood and fire do not co-exist safely; and on an aesthetic level, wood is undesirable as it tends to absorb, rather than to reflect, light. However, it is not surprising that many wooden candlesticks have been made in heavily forested parts of the world such as America, Great Britain, Austria and Scandinavia where wood is the most readily available material.

Many large, heavily carved candlesticks were made for use in churches, or in great castle halls. The candle would be equally large and was sometimes protected with an iron socket. Generally, they are very ornate, the wood is painted and gilded, very much like heavy picture frames. These were most common in Italy and Spain and similar ones were still being made until the 1900s.

In complete contrast are the small, straight shafts set on square bases which have narrow discrete bands of inlay around the top and bottom. These were made in Holland, Germany and Austria where the craft of wood-carving still flourishes.

When buying inlaid sticks, or those with marquetry designs or veneer, look carefully to see that all the pieces are in place. Unless done at home, such fine repairs can often cost more than the original object.

Beautifully turned oak candlestick, height 13 inches, possibly American, c. 1880. It is impossible to date wood with much certainty, but there are signs of natural wear on this candlestick in the light patches showing where the duster rubbed during polishing.

Chinese brass chambersticks

The simple vertical design of a candlestick presents an opportunity for symbolism and design motifs representative of a particular country or era.

Hence, the Corinthian columns, urns and floral swags represent English neo-classical design, the spiral, barley-sugar and baluster twists represent the English period of cabinet-making of 1660-1700 and reproductions of that period, and flowers are used by the Chinese to represent—among many things in their highly-symbolic designs—the seasons. The lotus depicted here is their summer flower.

At the end of the 19th century the Art Nouveau period was a reflection of Japanese influence on European craftsmen in every art form. But gradually it developed its own style and although oriental techniques and designs remained paramount, both Art Nouveau and the Arts and Crafts Movement grew into distinctive western idioms.

There is a hint of Art Nouveau design in these particular candle-holders, although the swirling plant forms are here subdued. The themes of life, growth, vigour and bursting energy were symbolized by organic plant life, not only as decorative motifs but as the whole shape of even basically practical articles. Flowers in particular were popular in China and in the West, but many plant forms were used.

With the enormous revival of trade in 19th-century China, Chinese artisans tried to copy imported objects, to make their own products more saleable in European and American markets. Here we have the copy of an originally oriental theme being put through the transformation of western fashion and being re-integrated by diligent but probably somewhat bewildered Chinese craftsmen.

Chinese brass chambersticks from c. 1900, height 4 inches, formed in the shape of lotus leaves with seed pods and showing the veins in the leaves.

Paktong and bell-metal

A number of misnomers and misunderstandings have crept into the body of information surrounding brass candlesticks. For instance, bell metal and gun metal are used to describe brass of reddish or pinkish tinge. Technically, bell and gun metal are both bronze—that is, alloys of copper and tin—that were used to make bells and cannons, and the terms should therefore be applied to items of bronze and not brass. The right-hand pair of candlesticks opposite have been called bell metal when in fact they are composed of copper and zinc and are, therefore, brass.

The left pair are of Paktong which has been referred to as 'white copper' (brass is sometimes termed 'yellow copper') and 'nickel brass'. Paktong is an alloy of copper, nickel and zinc. Although similarly constituted to brass, it looks more like silver than anything else. Imported from China into England from about 1750 to the end of that century, it was made most frequently into candlesticks. Few people are aware that these candlesticks exist, but they are of great interest to discerning collectors. Not only does Paktong look like silver, it is hard and tough, does not corrode as do other metals, and stays polished longer. When struck it gives a clear, bell-like musical tone.

Most frequently found candlestick styles in Paktong are variations of Corinthian columns. The colour of the metal varies slightly from item to item, from a white to a yellowish silver, depending on the amounts used of each constituent.

Compared with silver and brass, Paktong candlesticks are rare, but they have been confused with so-called 'German silver' which, although also an alloy of copper, nickel and zinc, was not introduced until the 19th century when it was much employed from c. 1845 as a base for electro-plated silver. Paktong ware has been found similarly coated, and some is still inadvertently hidden from the collector in this way. German silver was, however, given imitation silver marks whereas Paktong was usually unmarked.

Paktong candlesticks were always cast and the roughness resulting from the casting was usually scraped or chiselled away.

The right-hand pair, height $7\frac{1}{2}$ inches, is 19th-century brass with the reddish tinge erroneously called 'bell metal'. The design is still reproduced today. Left is a pair of late-18th-century Paktong candlesticks in the style of neo-classical Corinthian columns so popular in this alloy.

Brass 1

More candlesticks have been made of brass than of any other material. From at least the 14th century to the present they have served in churches, public buildings, and the home. Styles have been reproduced time and time again, often by the same methods. Collecting is therefore both rewarding, because there is a large choice available at reasonable prices, and hazardous, because age can be very difficult to judge.

Brass is an alloy of copper and zinc. Latten was an early type of pre-16th-century brass made by the methods then known, that is from copper melted with a zinc ore called calamine. Zinc as we know it was not known as a metal until the beginning of the 16th century.

Before the end of the 17th century the stem and nozzle were made of one mass of solid brass, cast and turned and fastened to a base by a screw or tenon. A hole in the side of the socket allowed a lever to be inserted for ejecting the candle stub. In order to conserve metal, a technique was developed whereby the stem and socket or nozzle were cast in two vertical halves, and brazed together and fastened to the base. This left the stem hollow so that ejectors could be inserted and thus ended the era of the hole-in-the-socket ejector. A rod with a button at each end was inserted which ran through the hollow stem and served to eject the candle. Cylindrical hollow stems were also made from hammered brass and a slot was fitted in the side of the stem for an ejector. About 1770 or 1780 an ordinary core-casting method was developed so that a hollow stem and nozzle could be produced in one.

Examples of the variety of 18th- and 19th-century brass candlesticks. The two tallest sticks in the rear, height 8½ inches, are not quite matching but date from c. 1780. The next pair, 6¾ inches high, are of a late-18th-century style but their late-Victorian date is signified by a thinness of design and metal. The two pairs in the foreground, height 4 inches and 3 inches, are tapersticks from c. 1820 and c. 1840 respectively, which held tapers for melting wax to seal letters.

Brass 2

Brass warmly reflects candlelight in a way that blends with oak furniture and rich, woven tapestries. The Georgian age of elegance brought with it a preference for precious silver, and brass was kept only for everyday use. With the fashion today once again tending towards pine, oak and country furniture, there are not enough brass candlesticks—particularly older ones—to go round.

The single candlestick in the left background of the illustration has the type of knops and swellings associated with silver of the George II period (also termed the Queen Anne period of silver, from 1700 to 1730) but is in fact much simpler, having no decoration—as befits the humbler material. The gentle petals or lobes of the base are repeated on the flange.

These early brass candlesticks are rapidly disappearing from the market just as early 18th-century silver and glass have been swallowed up into private collections. But these and earlier forms peculiar to brass—when available—are only a fraction of the price of 18th-century silver, especially if one aims to collect single sticks rather than pairs.

Splendid 18th- and 19th-century church candlesticks are also available to collectors at prices many can afford, as they are not yet greatly sought after.

Some 18th- and 19th-century brass candlesticks. Background, left, early Georgian in style with a petal base and flange, height 9½ inches and dating from c. 1720. Back right, a Gothic-style church candlestick, height 20 inches, bought in Majorca and dating from 1860-80. In the foreground, a pair of Victorian Gothic church candlesticks, 10 inches high and dating from 1880-90.

Brass 3

Brass candlesticks have been made in the familiar socket form from at least the 14th century. Up to the end of the 17th century, when the vogue for silver began, brass candlesticks had been developing in styles of their own. But at that time silver styles were imitated in brass and other materials. However, a certain amount of individuality remained and, unlike silver sticks, brass candlesticks were rarely ornamented beyond the shapes of the mouldings or modest beading and fluting. Moreover, the simple straight cylindrical stems, a type found largely in brass, continued to be produced during the 18th and 19th centuries.

As the candlestick developed during the 15th century, the stem was elaborated by the addition of mouldings or knops—probably to catch the candle wax—and the base deepened for the same purpose. Early in the 16th century a separate wax-pan appeared part way up the stem and by the 17th century this was in common use. Towards the end of that century, however, the wax-pan took up a position at the nozzle where it remained from then on, either as a flange on the nozzle or a detachable drip-pan. About this time, concurrent with silver beginning to dominate fashion, brass candlesticks began to take on national characteristics which in the 18th century were quite distinctive.

The most influential 18th-century silver designs on brass candlesticks were the simple baluster shapes of the early-Georgian period with small bulges along the stem and pretty lobed bases and flanges and the more austere neo-classical Adam period late in the century, featuring classical columns and elongated vase shapes. The more plastic, swirling and ornamented rococo was imitated less. These styles did at times merge in the same item.

In the 19th century, brass candlesticks developed round, oblong and small square bases and an infinite variety of knop shapes along the stems. The overall tendency was towards thicker, heavier-looking candlesticks.

Selection of brass candlesticks, height 10 inches, of styles made from the early 19th century to the present. These were made about 1820 except for the pair with the diamond-shaped knop which, although of a 19th-century design, are modern reproductions.

Brass 4

In America the materials most commonly used for candlesticks through the years have been iron, glass, and brass. Candlesticks of both iron and brass were made there, and also imported from Europe, but as these were humble metals such pieces were unmarked as to maker, date or country of origin, and are thus difficult to attribute with certainty.

Tin was also used for candlesticks—but, like iron ones, vast numbers must have simply rusted away before collector interest was sufficient to aid their preservation.

The wire or cage type of simple holder which can be raised or lowered is still found and other metal candlesticks had various kinds of socket raisers and plungers to eject the candle.

The straight-sided, cylindrical 'hog scraper' candle-holder, which was made in both brass and iron, was so named because the sharp-edged base made it popular in rural areas for scraping bristles from hogs after slaughtering.

During the period 1730 to 1750 candlesticks were both imported and made locally in America in increasing numbers. The so-called 'Queen Anne' style popular then is the most sought after in brass because of the simple elegance and delicate design of these candlesticks. Along with other antiques of the period, 'Queen Anne' brass candlesticks, British- or American-made, are out of reach for many collectors, although it is still possible to acquire single candlesticks for reasonable sums.

Pairs dating from the late 18th century and the 19th century, such as those pictured here, have yet to be fully appreciated, but the smaller ones, in particular, make admirable substitutes for the venerated 'Queen Anne' candlesticks.

When concentric circles are seen faintly on the bases, as here, they can be indications of two quite distinct manufacturing methods: casting and smoothing off the rough castings on a lathe, used in both early candlesticks and those of recent manufacture; or spinning thin sheets of brass into shape over a mould invented in America by W. H. Haydn in 1851. This pair is cast.

Although bought in America it is impossible to say with confidence whether this pair of brass candlesticks, height 12 inches, was made in the United States or England. The style of the knops is early 19th century.

Sconces

A sconce is a bracket candlestick attached to a wall. It usually consists of a back-plate with one or two arms extending from it with candle-holders on the end. Sconces are found mostly in brass, wood, silver, ormolu, glass and wrought iron.

They were in use on the European continent by the beginning of the 16th century. English wall sconces were made of metal until the late 17th century when they were often fashioned from wood and gilded. As a class they are highly ornamental, in keeping with the prevailing design of their day, but giving opportunity for skilful handiwork and creative embellishments.

Sconces held the main source of light in the smaller rooms of the period (roughly 1660-1714) and were important in the supplementing of light by chandeliers in the main rooms of middle- and upper-class homes. At this time, the sconce made with a metal or mirror back-plate to reflect the light into the room was at the height of popularity. The beautifully chased silver and brass examples are much sought after by collectors and are rather scarce and expensive but there are still a number of bracket-type wall candlesticks of brass, ormolu (brass or bronze which is gilded or covered with a gold-coloured lacquer), wood and wrought iron from the Georgian and Victorian periods available to the collector.

A cheap, attractive alternative is the piano candlestick of carved wood, wrought iron or brass from the late-Victorian and Edwardian periods when so many families regarded the piano as a necessary addition to the home. The pianos themselves have been destroyed wholesale, but the candle-holders, still used at that time to illuminate the music, have often survived and can be bracketed to the wall.

Brass piano candle-holders used as wall sconces. The top pair are late-Victorian, combining neo-classical Grecian fluted columns with rococo scrolls. The double 'sconce' below is one of a pair of Edwardian or earlier holders of Art Nouveau design. They all have the advantage of swivelling to different positions.

Brass 5

The vast majority of antique brass candlesticks available to collectors were made after about 1770, when increasing wealth brought about a huge demand for candlesticks and, at the same time, new methods of manufacturing enabled them to be provided at reasonable prices. Brass candlesticks were made more quickly and easily by casting the stem and socket in one complete piece and brazing it to the foot. Later on the entire candlestick could be cast in one piece.

A great challenge awaits the collector of late 18th- and 19th-century brass candlesticks. If he is prepared to compare methods of manufacture with styles and, through the constant handling of examples, to make himself familiar with the infinite varieties, he may eventually be able to do what few have achieved, date them with assurance.

Brassware of the late period has not had the attention that it deserves. Therefore, there are no rules for dating that can substitute for pure experience in handling. It is said that a rough grainy feel left inside the base from the casting can indicate a recent date; it is also said that this indicates a Georgian date before improved methods of casting left a smoother finish. However, it is also true that in earlier Georgian times the founder finished off his candlesticks by scraping the inside of rough castings to leave a smooth finish and this could be mistaken for a similar smooth finish left by later improved casting methods.

One sign of recent manufacture is a sharpness to edges—of bases, flanges etc. Constant use, handling and polishing tend to round off edges. The result of this confusion of techniques is that it is difficult to give hard-and-fast rules for dating. However, since collectors will probably be prepared to pay more for antique candlesticks than for late-19th- and 20th-century reproductions, the best help in dating lies in looking, touching and making mistakes. Experience, as always, is a hard teacher.

Cast-brass candlesticks, height 8 inches, of an 18th-century style, possibly French. The thinness of the stems suggests an Edwardian version of an 18th-century design. Cast brass is easily reproduced and it is difficult for the novice to distinguish the old from the new.

Open twist

One of the fascinating aspects of brass is the dual role it has played throughout history. Not only is the gold-coloured metal attractive for decorative use—as in candlesticks—but it was, and is, a prime material of industry.

Queen Elizabeth I, in her attempts to make her country more self-sufficient, ordered the making of brass so that England could provide her own armaments. During the English Civil War brass candlesticks were melted down to aid the war effort and later, during the Restoration of 1660, they were melted down to be made into newly fashionable shapes.

One of the designs of this period was the open double barley-sugar twist, a favourite technique for showing off the wood-turner's skill. The design was soon to be used in metals and has been much imitated in 19th- and 20th-century brass when late-17th-century styles returned to fashion. Such candlesticks as those shown here are unlikely to be earlier than Victorian and could very easily have been made within the last few years.

At some point in the 19th century brass candlesticks began to be made in one piece from a single mould but this method is difficult to distinguish from the alternative which continued to be used, consisting of casting the base separately and soldering to the stem or joining by long screws.

Unfortunately this later period is very hard to identify as to origin; styles in England and America copied each other almost instantaneously, and goods travelled in huge shipments across the ocean. A manufacturer's mark helps, or sometimes, if the stick can be unscrewed, clues can be found inside. Occasionally, too, it is possible to locate a manufacturer's design book which has the exact pattern, but even then it could easily be a copy of another factory's output! The most important clue to date and quality is the patina of old, well-cared-for metal combined with good design and sharp detail.

Brass open-twist candlesticks, height 10 inches, American 20th-century reproduction of a late-17th-century wooden style.

Brass chambersticks

Chambersticks were used in bedrooms and for travelling, their wide pans and low height providing the maximum stability for carrying light from room to room or for illuminating a coach. The broad grease-pan was in some cases deepened like a bowl or flattened like a plate, but it could also be round, square or octagonal in shape. Chambersticks were made in all materials, but the most common was brass.

The chamberstick with its squat central socket for the candle was carried by looped or long flat handles and sometimes had feet. Frequently they were furnished with cone-shaped extinguishers, though scissor extinguishers were also used; these came separately, frequently furnished with their own trays to rest on.

Chambersticks were in use in England and America well into the 20th century in rural areas where there was no electricity. They are doubtless still used in many parts of the world.

Shades were sometimes provided for use in draughts, leading to the development of the so-called 'hurricane' lamp, in which a tall cylindrical glass shade was placed over the candle. The shade rested on the pan of the chamberstick or on a collar or 'basket' specially constructed to take the shade and help make it secure.

A certain type of wooden chamberstick that could be unscrewed for travelling and reassembled for use was known as a 'Brighton Bun' and probably dates from the 19th century in England.

Two 19th-century English brass chambersticks of types known from the 18th century. The one in the foreground, diameter 6 inches, with a knob in a slot to eject the candle stub, has a slight rococo feel in the shaping at the base of the candle-holder and in the handle. The one in the background, diameter 6¾ inches, has lost its original snuffer but a substitute of appropriate style is shown behind the scissor snuffer.

Church brass

From the mid-1800s onwards an enthusiastic following developed for the medieval designs of Augustus Pugin and William Morris and the writings of John Ruskin. This resulted in a trend towards Gothic revival styles which is mirrored in the church candlesticks shown here.

Pugin designed large quantities of stained glass, furniture, wallpapers, textiles and metalwork, including candlesticks and jewellery. The stained glass and metalwork were largely designed for churches which he considered aptly suited to the Gothic style. He wrote in 1836: 'The great test of beauty is the fitness of design for the purpose for which it was intended'. Pugin, Morris and Ruskin were the main inspiration behind what later became the Art Nouveau movement in Europe, Great Britain and America.

The Gothic revival was considerably older than Pugin, however, beginning really in about the mid-1700s as an alternative to Georgian styles. But in Pugin's time (1812-52) there was the added impetus of a religious movement to 'Christianize' church architecture.

Church candlesticks such as those pictured here, though of commercialized Gothic form and not products of the leading exponents of design of the movement, are nevertheless well made and extremely decorative. Ecclesiastical antiques, except for paintings, are not yet widely collected, but as religious fervour diminishes in many parts of the world, church antiques are bound to provide historical interest for younger generations.

Candlesticks often formed an important part of the church decoration, their styles remaining consistent over the years, except for subtle changes in proportion and motifs. A collection of church candlesticks would require a lot of space since some floor-standing sticks reach 6 feet at least.

Brass church candlesticks, height 13 inches, c. 1880, in the medieval style. Throughout history, the precious silver, gold and jewelled candlesticks supplied to rich churches and cathedrals of the day were imitated in less wealthy congregations with brass.

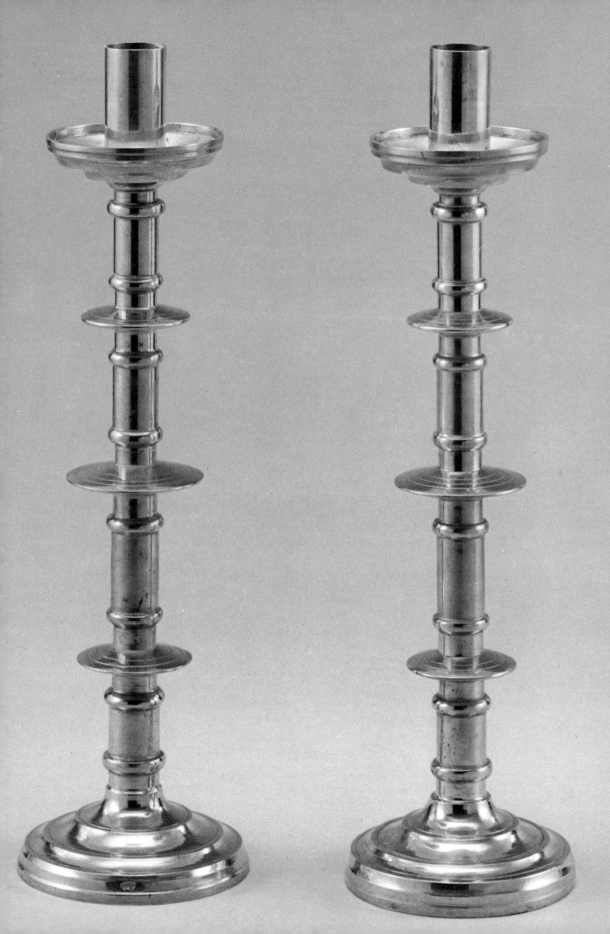

Menorah

The menorah or seven-branched candelabrum is the symbol of the State of Israel and for centuries has been used in synagogues and homes of Jewish people throughout the world. Menorahs are thus fairly plentiful and, being impressive and distinctive candelabra, are attractive to Jew and non-Jew alike.

Originally the form is thought to have derived from the Middle-Eastern Tree of Life, so often represented in Middle-Eastern and Jewish art. The sacred tree is reflected in the Torah, which 'is the tree of life to them that lay hold upon her' (Proverbs 3: 16-18).

The menorah is descended from the original seven-branched candelabrum of the tabernacle which perished when the temple was destroyed, traditionally to be seen again on the Day of Judgement. Not until the 12th century did Jews begin to create candelabra for actual use in synagogues and later for the home—before that, they appeared only pictorially. Menorahs are found pictured in mosaics, decorations of the synagogue, on material relating to the Jewish festival commemorating the rededication of the temple (Hanukkah), on seals, medals, wine cups, amulets, coins, in sacred manuscripts and books, on glass and on lamps.

From earliest times the number seven has been related to the lamp, and the first seven-bracket lamps were probably made of pottery. According to rabbinical literature the seven lights represent the seven days of creation with the Sabbath symbolized by the centre light. The number has also been interpreted as representing the seven continents and seven traditional heavens.

In the 12th century the candelabrum which appeared in synagogues was nine-branched, but by about the 16th century seven branches became traditional and remain so to this day.

Menorahs are usually made in brass or silver. There have been a number of American silversmiths (such as Myer Myers) who have made all kinds of Jewish ritual objects including menorahs and Sabbath candlesticks, with basic patterns in the style of the period. But manufactured objects range from traditional designs to very modern Israeli interpretations. From the 12th century to the present, they have often served as instruments for the highest artistic expression. Their design over the centuries, not forgetting those of modern times, would make a fascinating study.

Brass menorah or seven-branched candelabrum, height 10 inches, symbol of the Jewish religion and the State of Israel. This American example, c. 1890, is of a traditional 17th-century design with knops along the branches.

Brass tablesticks

As gas, electric and oil lighting became more and more common in Victorian and Edwardian homes, the function of the candlestick greatly diminished in importance. It became purely decorative, in many cases reduced to the role of providing a cheap souvenir or gift. However, for the dining table, candlelight remained (and still is) the festive asset which makes ordinary supper into dinner, and dinner into a party.

A great many were made to decorate the table, sitting among sprigs of evergreen or holly. Such small candlesticks as those pictured here are suited to such purposes as, without handles they are impractical for carrying from room to room.

The water-lily motif, which often occurs in Art Nouveau objects and designs of the period, here appears less convoluted than usual; the candlesticks look more like pure stars, perhaps meant for use during the Christmas season. Such a purely decorative function would never have been possible during the many centuries in which daylight, candlelight and firelight were the main sources of illumination.

There was also the Victorian delight in a cluster (or what we might call a clutter) of small tables covered with objects; small sticks were made as little objets d'art, to be displayed together with a box, a glass animal or two, a match-holder, a figurine and three or four little bowls and vases.

Such candlesticks have a particular charm, and were particularly well adapted to novelty shapes and designs. An interesting collection could be built up concentrating on those measuring 5 inches or 6 inches, or less.

In America, brass candlesticks were for many years virtually non-existent unless imported from England or the continent of Europe. An Act of the English Parliament of 1699 forbade manufacturing in the American colonies and required that raw materials be brought from the New World and made into manufactured goods that were then supplied back to the colonies. In the 18th century, brass candlesticks from Birmingham, England, were familiar in the colonies—and for a long time after American independence.

American brass candlesticks, height 4 inches, c. 1890. Although they are the size of chambersticks or bed-lamps, the absence of handles and the water-lily design stylized into star-shapes suggests a purely decorative role.

Ormolu

One could argue that no candlestick collection would be complete without an example of French ormolu. The gold and gilt of the courts of Louis XIV (1643-1715) and Louis XV (1715-74) live on in the elaborate confections of rococo ormolu candelabra that continued to be reproduced throughout the 19th century.

Ormolu is gilded or gold-painted bronze, brass and sometimes tin, and was much used for mounts to embellish French and French-influenced furniture. At the foundation of rococo was an asymmetrical use of natural forms such as foliage, flowers, rocks and shells. There were few straight lines. Curves in C and S shapes were predominant.

Throughout the 1700s and 1800s ormolu sconces and candelabra were made in England and on the continent of Europe, but rarely does one find candlesticks as the style was too flamboyant to be confined to a single vertical.

Ormolu does wear away in the most vulnerable spots through the years and examples are often found which have been painted over; the sharp-eyed collector may be fortunate enough to find a once-expensive item now selling for very little, due to a heavy coating of unaesthetic, peeling enamel. Another favourite 'touching-up' technique is to paint over the worn ormolu with brassy gold paint which equally destroys the original appeal.

Ormolu can be regilded but this is an expensive process. It is usually best left in a state of natural wear with, perhaps, a modest cleaning.

Ormolu candlesticks were often combined with crystal or porcelain. Because of their rich decoration they seemed to be especially vulnerable to the craze for conversion into bedside lamps, and were often clumsily adapted and enlarged with wooden bases and gilt-wood finials. It is worth while looking carefully at such unattractive bastard concoctions, since sometimes the reward is a small gem in the middle which can be restored to its original appearance.

Ormolu candelabrum, height 12 inches, probably French, dating from the 19th century. Floral, leaf, and scroll shapes employed in this asymmetrical manner are typical of the rococo style in which most ormolu candle-holders, of gilded or gold-lacquered bronze or brass, were made.

Nickel on brass

The most universally desired of all candlesticks have always been silver—even more so than gold, as so few were made of the more precious metal. Silver styles have set the standards for all others. Those who could afford to own silver candlesticks did so and those who could not preferred close imitations.

It is not surprising, therefore, that pewter was for long 'the poor man's silver' as, when new, it closely resembled the shining gleam of silver. Then, when processes for coating base metals with thin layers of silver were developed from the mid-18th century onwards, objects made in this way were much sought after.

Brass and copper could hardly be mistaken for silver but were nevertheless fashioned in the same styles. Later they formed the base onto which thin layers of silver were fused, in silver-plating.

When nickel was discovered on the site of silver mines in Saxony, it was developed in an alloy to produce a grey or whitish-coloured material to be used on its own or to be plated over. One of its great advantages as a base for plating was that when the silver wore thin, the nickel did not show through.

Nickel plated onto brass is rare but makes a harmonious marriage as the two base metals are similar in colour tone. Nickel on its own is difficult to fuse with other metals and must therefore be alloyed with metals such as zinc.

So-called 'German silver' used in imitation of silver, and also as a base for electro-plating, is a mixture of nickel, zinc and copper.

Unusual brass candlesticks in that they are nickel-plated. They are 8 inches high, probably English, c. 1890. The design is 19th-century, but continued into the present century.

Cut glass

Glass candlesticks were in use from the mid-17th century. At first they were made in one piece and tended to follow silver and brass shapes. Later a glass or metal holder was inserted to catch the grease and save the nozzle from cracking under the candle flame. Later still, nozzles were made with metal mounts and screwed into the stem, and sometimes were provided with metal save-alls to place in the glass nozzle as an added safeguard. A detachable nozzle was obviously practical as it could be replaced, but some candlesticks continued to be made in one piece throughout the 18th and 19th centuries.

The 18th century began with a fashion for very plain candlesticks, hollow blown and looking rather like the hollow silver ones. Then came fancier effects, such as Silesian stems, air twist, opaque stems and faceted stems. During the Adam period there was increasing elaboration seen in the urn-shaped pendant drop centre-pieces and the cut-glass chandeliers dripping with festoons of faceted pendants. The simple Adam style was represented by a type of fluted column stem and square, terraced feet similar to silver candlesticks of the period.

When English glass-makers were burdened with the glass excise taxes of 1777, 1781, and 1787, some production shifted to Ireland where such taxes were not in force until 1825 and there was more or less free trade with England. This was the period when heavy cut glass was much favoured, and Irish glass thus became famous for this technique.

Cut glass was unfashionable during the late 1850s, the 60s and 70s, partly because pressed glass imitations helped to turn the élite against it and partly because it was considered wasteful and, to use John Ruskin's word for it, 'barbaric'. But it returned to favour in the 1880s and 90s and continues to be popular today.

Cuts are made by using an iron wheel fed with an abrasive such as sand and the facets are then polished on a wheel or by immersing the item in an acid bath—a later technique.

On the left are cut-glass candlesticks and in the foreground press-moulded, both probably late-19th century. The simple country-made pottery candlestick on the right, height 4 inches, is probably German.

Venetian glass

Glass-making was well established in Venice by the 13th century. To prevent fire, glass furnaces were moved to the nearby island of Murano in about 1295. Early Venetian glass had strong jewel colours and enamelled decoration, but about 1460 the formula for 'cristallo' was developed. This new kind of soda glass was extremely light, easy to work, and very clear—the nearest thing to rock crystal yet achieved (hence the name).

Imagination matched techniques, and Venetian artistry in glass became world-famous. Fantastic shapes, swirling stems, feather-light decoration, animals, plants, flowers, ships—there seemed no limit to their ingenuity. Useful drinking glasses and candlesticks were enriched far beyond their functional limits to become decorative showpieces.

Venice knew the value of skilled men, and glass-workers were forbidden to leave. None-the-less, increasing numbers escaped and travelled to Germany, France, England, the Netherlands, Spain and Portugal, bringing their knowledge with them.

The fashion for cut and wheel-engraved glass in the 18th century marked the end of Venice's greatest period, since these new crafts relied on the heavy, stronger lead or flint glass which was developed in England around 1670. But the wide scope of colours and elaborate glass-on-glass techniques the Venetians used remain an important influence, returning with special force towards the end of the 19th and early 20th centuries.

In France, England and America, millefiori was adapted and used extensively for making paperweights, door knobs, door stops, inkwells, and candlestick bases.

The kaleidoscope of colours, from simple white 'milk' to triple layers of gem colours, with glittering specks or fine white threads spun like lace—all this delighted the newly-affluent middle class. Americo-Venetian glass-makers were particularly inventive— Nicholas Lutz was an early devotee, Louis Tiffany took the Art Nouveau forms and married them to lustrous iridescent surfaces, and Frederick Carder of Steuben not only redeveloped Venetian colourings but achieved simple, elegant shapes which echoed the best of Venetian craftsmanship.

Venice itself has continued to produce fine glass, and the factories of Murano are still a tourist 'must'.

The flower was a favourite Art Deco motif but not usually in such a softly-rendered, realistic form as this 1930s Venetian glass candlestick, height 7 inches, made of clear and amber glass.

Blue glass

Techniques for colouring glass have been much the same throughout the history of glass-making. Metallic oxides are added to the composition, cobalt or copper producing blues, gold or copper producing reds.

Blue was the earliest colour used in glass-making and some of the most famous of all glass has been made in shades of blue, e.g. Venetian glass, the Roman Portland Vase and so-called Bristol blue glass.

During the 18th and early 19th centuries the variety of coloured glass in England and America was almost entirely restricted to blue, amethyst and green, but of the three blue was by far the most popular, used not only for individual objects such as glasses, decanters, bottles and candlesticks but traditionally as the lining for silver filigree tableware—bowls, salts, pots etc. What little elaborate coloured glass there was came from Bohemia and east Germany until the repeal of the excise tax in 1845 (based on the weight of glass used) allowed English glass centres such as Stourbridge and Gateshead to develop in all possible ways—glass on glass, glass within glass, glass intermingled—and in colours of ruby, rose, blue, green, amber, gold and amethyst.

Pressed glass, developed in America and England from the 1820s onwards, provided buyers with many sturdy, inexpensive candlesticks now available to the collector of modest means. Early designs were often drawn from traditional motifs and themes as with the candlesticks pictured here. The bases obviously imitate those of classical columns, but the stems could be described as either twisted columns or barley-sugar twists like those used in early-English furniture. These twists were revived by the Victorians and Edwardians, and appear on furniture, many candlestick stems, clock cases and other ornaments.

Moulds were made into which the glass was pressed. When the sides of the moulds were taken away, tell-tale seams were left which, in the more expensive items, were filed away to give the appearance of hand-blown glass. One can easily detect the seams on the pair pictured here.

Pressed glass candlesticks, height 10 inches, of peacock-blue glass. These are American, c. 1890, and draw on two styles popular at that time: the classical, based on Greek and Roman traditions, and the barley-sugar twist.

Bohemian glass

Bohemian glass-making led the world during the 17th and 18th centuries, particularly in the arts of engraving and cutting, and it was exported all over the world.

However, English and Irish cut glass achieved fame and popularity after the mid-18th century. The lavish use of glass cut into deep facets in the shape of diamonds, stars, flutes, steps, ovals, rosettes, etc. in England and Ireland during the Regency period set the styles for subsequent revivals and represented a high point in a craft in which Irish glass, in particular, became synonymous with splendid cut glass. Candlesticks were made in detachable sections allowing easy replacement of broken parts.

In the 19th century, Bohemian factories so successfully adopted the English and Irish style of heavy cutting that it continues today as one of their successful export lines. The candlesticks shown here reflect the post-Regency fashion for flat-cutting or surface-slicing in a vertical pattern.

Bohemia and other German-speaking areas also became famous for coloured glass. Towards the end of the 17th century Johann Kunckel of Potsdam produced a deep ruby-red colour which is much sought after by collectors. A later type of ruby-red glass was popular in the 19th century when it was made in Bohemia and in England at Stourbridge.

Clear glass that was stained or given an outer coating of ruby-red was a popular product about 1850 from Bohemian and English glass-making firms. The stain or coating was cut through to reveal the colourless glass beneath, which could then be left clear, painted, gilded, or engraved.

Pair of Bohemian glass candlesticks, c. 1840, cut in a flat vertical pattern fashionable after the Regency period. An outer coating of ruby-red glass has been cut through to make an attractive decoration on clear glass. There is an additional embellishment in the band of engraving around the stems.

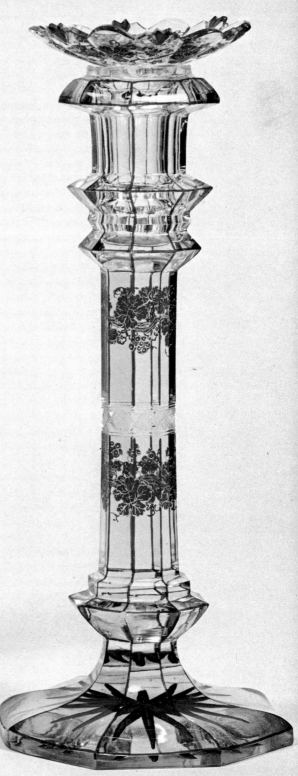

Heisy glass

The United States, although a comparatively young country, is a rich source of collecting items. The decorative arts have, in large measure, been derivative of European precedents, but, in the field of glass, America is justifiably proud of leading the way during the 19th and 20th centuries in the development of a large and varied amount of new techniques, shapes, colours and textures.

By the 1900s there were a few firms who continued to specialize in producing very fine glass. Since this lovely material was particularly effective in candlesticks, tall crystal-clear sticks were produced in many simple shapes and patterns.

One of the many firms producing glass that is now fervently collected was the Heisy factory, located in Newark, Ohio. From the late 1800s to the mid-1950s it provided pressed, etched, coloured, and silver overlay glass that was remarkable for its almost flawless clarity. Besides commercial table glass, it manufactured a wide range of glass animals and other highly collectable items. Such is the interest in Heisy glass that there have been auctions devoted entirely to it.

A mark was sometimes incorporated in the glass in the form of a diamond with an 'H' in the centre. At other times, in common with many modern glass manufacturers, the firm used paper stickers rather than imprinting the mark in the glass.

These neo-classical glass candlesticks, c. 1900, show the almost flawless crystal clarity for which the Newark, Ohio, Heisy glass firm is noted and which is the delight of collectors. They are 10 inches high, with six-sided stems and bases and with flowers etched on the stems.

Pressed glass

Glass objects have been made in moulds from time immemorial. A kind of hard moulded glass was made around the 13th century BC and possibly even earlier. When glass-blowing was developed in the 1st century BC, the technique of blowing into wooden moulds to make a number of identical shapes was developed almost simultaneously. Blown mould glass remained the only way of mechanical production for the next 1800 years.

During the 1820s in America mechanical pressing was introduced, making real mass-production possible and revolutionizing the glass industry.

The method involves pouring molten glass manually or mechanically into a patterned mould; a plunger is rammed into the mould, forcing the glass into all parts and impressing the pattern on it. The plunger itself is smooth, so that the article is patterned only on the outside, in contrast to glass blown into a mould, which creates a reverse pattern on the inside surface.

Early American pressed glass candlesticks often had free-blown stems, with only the bases pressed. The Boston and Sandwich Glass Company of Massachusetts is always associated with early pressed glass, but between 1829 and 1850 there were at least 16 other factories in the USA producing on a commercial scale. In England pressed glass came in about the mid-19th century.

Early 19th-century pressed glass tended to imitate the cut glass so popular during the Regency period. Then came the famous 'lacy' period of about 1825 to 1850 during which highly intricate all-over patterns on stippled and relief dotted backgrounds were made possible by the introduction of iron moulds, which could be carved in great detail.

Lacy glass was imitated in England in the 1860s, 70s and 80s in the use of stippled and dotted grounds.

It is worth keeping an eye out for pressed commemorative glass candlesticks, for where a date or event is marked the value of an item tends to increase. Commemorative pressed glass is, however, still extremely inexpensive and candlesticks as well as other items could be well worth collecting in terms of future appreciation.

Examples of American pressed glass candlesticks: the small clear candlestick, height 5 inches, c. 1830, contains a 'lacy pattern' on the base characterized by a stippled and dotted background. The blue candlestick, height 8 inches, c. 1825, is based on late 18th-century design.

Satin glass

Among the immense variety of glass types perfected in the 19th century was Satin Glass, also known as 'Mother-of-Pearl Satin Glass', 'Pearl Ware' and 'Verre de Soie', 'Velvet' and 'Watered Silk', of which there are a number of patterns and colours.

Basically the technique involved trapping air within the glass so that symmetrical patterns such as stripes or knops could occur. A gather of glass was blown into a pattern mould and then covered by another gather of glass which trapped air between the two layers. Another method was to line a heated mould with glass tubes and, by blowing a bubble of glass into this mould, catch the tubes into the body of the vessel to produce swirling stripes.

The technique used to make the black Satin Glass pictured here was probably simply to colour the glass with metallic oxide and treat the surface with acid, thus dulling it. Black has not been a very popular colour for glass or candlesticks, perhaps because of its association with witchcraft and funerals. Two notable exceptions were the opaque black glass made at Haughton Green near Manchester in the early 17th century and black Hyalith glass made in Bohemia from 1820. However, black was sometimes used as enamel decoration on coloured Satin Glass, especially on blues, pinks and ambers.

Coloured glass was at its zenith during the 19th century, with makers vying with each other to discover new methods of production.

Patents for various types of Satin Glass were taken out between 1857 and 1889 in England, France and America. Much later, Satin Glass of cheaper quality was made in France and Bohemia.

By the end of the 19th century Satin Glass was made by all the important glass houses in America and England, so this makes an easily collectable field, and Satin Glass candlesticks show a correspondingly wide range of form and decoration.

Black Satin Glass candlestick, height 9 inches, made by the Cambridge Glass Company, Cambridge, Mass., about 1900. As black is a rather unusual colour in candlesticks, it may be that this was made in imitation of the popular black basalt of Wedgwood and other ceramic firms.

Jade glass

Glass objects were made in imitation of jade as early as the 4th century B.C. in China. The Venetians also developed coloured glasses of all kinds including jade, quartz etc. The Chinese continued to imitate carved stones and materials during their prolific period of glass-blowing in the 18th century. By the mid-19th century the clear crystal which had been popular for so long was giving way to the newly fashionable, brilliantly coloured glasses from Bohemia. This was particularly true after the great 1851 exhibition, and English and American craftsmen began to develop intricate formulae and methods which resulted in the most amazing array of colours and finishes.

Jade glass had already been made by Stevens & Williams of Stourbridge, England, and the Steuben Glass Works of New York had inherited this from Frederick Carder who worked in both firms. He came to America around 1900, was co-founder of the Steuben Works in 1903 and later, when Corning Glass bought the works, he became Art Director. Carder was responsible for a number of other ingenious techniques of glass-making, including Silk Glass (Verre de Soie), Aurene, Cluthra, Moss Agate, Millefiori and Bubbly Glass. He also cased or overlaid the coloured 'jade' glass with a translucent white glass (called alabaster) and engraved through it. Occasionally, jade glass was given a satin or dull finish. A rose-coloured jade glass that was also popular in America was Rosaline.

In imitating the jewel-like quality of jade, Carder added oxides to translucent white glass in order to produce the many colours of jade, and its soft, almost 'soapy', glow.

Many other glassworks imitated Carder's work, or developed colour formulae of their own. These include Victor Durand in the 1920s and 30s and Robert Gunderson in the 1940s, who copied the earlier Peach Blow and Burmese Glass.

Candlesticks were always a popular glass product and were made in almost all known blown glass and pressed glass patterns.

Green jade glass candlesticks, 1920-30, height 10 inches, made to imitate the jewel-like quality of jade, a product of the Cambridge Glass Works, Cambridge, Ohio. Frederick Carder was the man largely responsible for this technique.

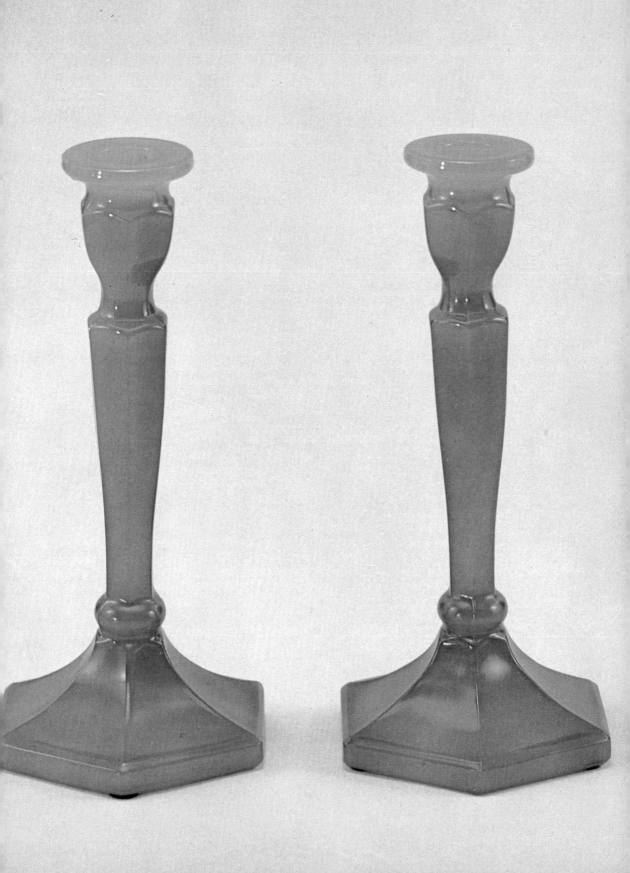

Mercury or silver glass

A Victorian novelty known as 'silver' or 'mercury' glass enjoyed great popularity and was particularly successful when used for candlesticks as it created the illusion of silver at a very much cheaper price. It was made in various parts of Europe and America from the mid-19th century and various techniques were patented.

F. Hale Thomson and E. Varnish applied silver mercury between two layers of glass, whereas Oscar Pierre Erard, a Frenchman living in England, and John Round patented a method for electro-depositing gold, silver, copper and other metallic designs on glass, as well as on pottery and porcelain. This technique involved painting a design on the glass with a special flux and firing it in a kiln. The article was then placed in a solution of the particular metal required and an electric current passed through the solution would deposit the metal on the glass.

In poor areas of the country silvered-glass candlesticks were often used in Victorian churches instead of silver. Such ornamental glass subsequently became popular for fairground prizes, often gaudily painted with flowers. Such a candlestick, undamaged and with the original silvering and paint intact, is likely to be an outstanding collector's item of the future if properly preserved in perfect condition.

Mercury or silver glass was made in the USA by the New England Glass Co., which received a patent in 1855 for making silvered-glass door knobs.

It is important, if buying for investment as well as pleasure, to ensure that glass objects are in perfect condition, unless they are exceedingly rare types which are worth paying a restorer to make good. Generally, the most that can be restored of a glass article is a chipped rim, or detachable parts such as nozzles or pendant lustres.

On the other hand, buying damaged pieces, if they are really cheap, is a very good method of self-instruction. All the descriptions in the world cannot match the benefit of holding a piece in your hands.

Don't ignore more modern glass—some fine pieces are still hand-blown even today in the same tradition, and good examples of the glass-blower's art are available.

American 'mercury' or 'silver' glass candlesticks. The single example, height 9 inches, dates from c. 1880 and the pair, height 5 inches, from c. 1900. 'Silver' is a misnomer as the metallic designs produced on glass of this category were also of other colours such as red.

Bohemian Hyalith glass lustres

'Lustres' are the cut-glass pendants that hang from 18th-century chandeliers and certain table candlesticks from the 18th century onwards. They did add 'lustre' or sparkle to the quality of candlelight by reflecting the light in the cut facets. From 1850 the term was applied to table candelabra with these pendants.

There are splendid expensive 18th-century table candlesticks or candelabra with these pendants and with bases or drums made of Wedgwood Jasper, or marble such as Bluejohn, and embellished with gilding. There are beautiful Regency clear cut-glass candlestick lustres and there are ornate, coloured 19th-century lustres such as the one pictured here.

A number of candle lustres were made in Ireland during the Regency period when the opulent use of glass was popular, but initially they made their appearance after about 1760. They might consist of, as in the photograph, a wide saucer with the candle socket in the centre and the lustres hanging from the edge of the saucer; or the holder might have no additional saucer, being simply a candle-stick with the lustres hanging from its rim. Early lustres were flat and pear-shaped; later they were longer and more attenuated.

One of a pair of Bohemian glass candlesticks or 'lustres', height 12 inches, c. 1870, of a type also made during the 19th century in England. It is of black glass called 'Hyalith' (the name also given to a sealing-wax-red glass invented in Bohemia) with white and blue flowered enamel decoration. The cut-glass lustres or pendants are of clear glass.

Enamel

English enamel objects were made from the 1750s to about 1830 at London workshops including Battersea, at Bilston and Wednesbury in South Staffordshire, and at Birmingham and Liverpool. Candlesticks were made from about 1770 after the Battersea factory had closed, and the term Battersea enamel applied to candlesticks is therefore a misnomer.

The technique involved fusing opacified glass (the enamel background in white or pale pastels) on thin copper and then hand-painting with bright enamel colours. Flowers, birds, landscapes, classical ruins, port scenes and commemorative inscriptions are among the decorations found on candlesticks. Often the basic design was printed on the candlestick and then hand-painted. The enamels were fired at high temperatures and their edges rimmed with gilt.

Before 1780 they were made in three parts and brazed together, but afterwards constructed in one piece. Styles generally followed silver prototypes such as the slender baluster shape, gently knopped and lobed as those in the photograph, or the Corinthian columns that dominated candlestick design from about 1765 to the end of the century under the influence of Robert Adam.

The same shapes continued to be made in the early 19th century, but less time and skill were employed in the making. Early sticks from the period about 1770-90 might have inset panels with scenes and landscapes and gilded enrichments, but rising costs required simpler designs after that. A more bulbous Victorian feel also crept into later candlesticks. All enamels of this period are growing more and more expensive and difficult to find, but the later products of the 19th century are still collectable, particularly in single sticks instead of pairs.

The firm of Samson of Paris copied the well-loved English enamels from the mid-19th century. These often fool new collectors and are now collected in their own right, though they should not command as high a price as the English originals.

English enamel candlesticks, height 9 inches, probably South Staffordshire, c. 1770, in simple Georgian style with slender baluster stem of tasteful knops and gently lobed base and flange to the candle socket. They are made in three sections, which dates them before 1780. The slight swirls on the base and the lobes are motifs of rococo design. The flutings on the lobes and the tasteful simple flowers are also typical of this period.

Plated silver 1

Electro-plated silver found a ready market in Great Britain and, even more, in the United States from the mid-19th century onwards. Its use for candlesticks as well as a multitude of other items has created a huge field for the collector. At the same time it presents hazards, as much antique silver-plating is very worn.

With Old (early) Sheffield Plate, the forerunner of electro-plating, the flashes of copper underlay can actually enhance an article, as this indicates that it has not been replated (see page 98). Conversely, if the silver is too well worn it may be worth replating, since Old Sheffield Plate is rare compared with electro-plated examples.

Old Sheffield Plate was made by fusing thin sheets of silver onto a copper base, which is then worked as is solid silver, whereas electro-plating is a much more mechanical method of plating on copper, or more usually on a white metal such as nickel which will not show through when the silver has rubbed off. The article is immersed in a solution containing particles of silver. An electric current passed through the solution results in the silver being electro-deposited on the object.

In England, the Birmingham firm of Elkington became well known in this field but also made fine silver. In America, Rogers and Mead, Rogers Brothers, Meriden Britannia Company and Reed and Barton were famous makers of early electro-plate.

The period of Old Sheffield Plate roughly spanned 100 years—up to the invention of electro-plating in 1838. Virtually all British silver or plated silver bears marks, required by law, by which one can ascertain dates, makers, place of origin and material used. In America, marking has been less consistent. When marks appear they are usually in the form of the maker's initials or full name possibly combined with an emblem.

During the early 1800s the word 'coin' appeared on American silverware indicating fineness equal to the high quality of the coinage. About the mid-19th century the word 'sterling' was used to indicate high-quality silver and during the present century the words 'coin', 'coin silver', 'sterling' and 'sterling silver' indicate the proper fineness of 925 parts fine silver to 75 parts fine copper within each 1000 parts. Sometimes the retail store also added their name. Neither silver plate nor solid silver carries a datemark, so that considerable research may be necessary to establish accurate information.

American electro-plated silver candlesticks, c. 1925, height 7 inches, unmarked. Although traditionally based on 18th-century neo-classical design, the six-sided facets of the stems, base and 'cheeks' of the nozzles have a modern geometrical feel.

Neo-classical silver

So much silver was melted down to finance the English Civil War fought between the forces of Cromwell and Charles II that very little exists from the period prior to the Restoration of the monarchy in 1660.

By the end of the 17th century a common type of candlestick was a rather short column, usually fluted but sometimes of the clustered Gothic type. There are examples from the period with distinct drip-pans, but for the most part they have shrunk to become part of the mouldings or advanced up the stem to surround the nozzle as a flange.

Early 18th-century styles were usually thick cast. The stems were baluster-shaped with gentle, tasteful mouldings creating vase shapes and with very little ornamentation except for fluting at the corners of the squarish bases and on the shoulders.

As the century advanced, so did the height and elaboration of candlesticks. Sets of up to a dozen were made for the grand families. The simple forms of the Queen Anne period gave way to the highly-ornamental rococo styles of the period 1730 to 1760 when English candlesticks designed by craftsmen such as French Huguenot silversmith Paul de Lamerie were alive with foliage, scrolls, swirls, gadroons and moulded decoration.

Fashions changed rather abruptly in the late 18th century when people tired of the rococo and news from the excavations at Pompeii and Herculaneum reached England. Greek architecture, popular through much of the history of design, was especially so under the influence of Robert Adam (1728-92). The Corinthian column from the Stuart era reappeared in a more authentic form as knowledge about classical designs advanced. Articles in silver, glass, ceramics and brass all underwent a classical revival as drapes, festoons, urns, fluted columns, pedestals, capitals, garlands, cherubs and cameos lent their forms to artefacts like candlesticks, candelabra and chandeliers. No other style for candlesticks has been so enthusiastically reproduced during the 19th and 20th centuries as that of the fluted Corinthian column.

The well-to-do Georgian household was well-provided with silver candelabra, chambersticks, tapersticks and candlesticks, all in Adam's shapes. They were designed so well that neo-classical forms continue to be popular, in pottery, silver, and glass, and they go well with the neo-classical furniture styles which have also adapted miraculously to modern living.

Reproduction silver candlesticks, height 4¾ inches, in the neo-classical style of a Corinthian column and hallmarked Chester 1907. The fluted column, stepped base with beading and capital with acanthus leaf decoration are typical.

Art Nouveau silver

Victorian silver candlesticks are not as plentiful as one might think. There seems to have been a temporary lull in silver candlestick manufacture from about 1830 to 1880, either because of the spread of gas and oil lighting or because the Victorian love of show led to a preference for elaborate candelabra on the dining-table. However, individual sticks became fashionable again, as they are even today for table displays and their attractive flickering light.

The best candlesticks and candelabra were cast into moulds rather than being die-stamped, which was a technique of stamping the design by machine on sheets of silver and then assembling the parts. Some were hand-made in sheet silver.

No sector of the art market has changed so radically as Victorian silver. Despised and rejected for most of this century, it is now in many cases overtaking in popularity the long-established Georgian silver. Victorian silver, like any other, is judged on the quality of its workmanship and the weight of the material. Until recently, Victorian pieces were out of favour but the profusion of historical styles that frequently became mixed in the same item, as well as the tendency to over-elaboration, is in such contrast to the plain functionalism of much modern ware that many collectors now take pleasure in owning these rich confections of a former age. There are also good copies of single styles such as rococo, and the highly original Art Nouveau silver is usually well designed and well made.

Liberty & Co.'s 'Cymric' silver range produced between about 1899 and the 1930s is still within reach of modest collectors and, like the company's 'Tudric' pewter, well worth having. Candlesticks were happily well in fashion by then.

Designs similar to those of Liberty Tudric Pewter were made, or perhaps it is more accurate to say that Tudric candlesticks and chambersticks similar to Cymric were made, as it is likely that pewter imitated the more fashionable and expensive silver.

Though not cheap, 'Cymric' silver was inexpensive in relation to other hand-made silver, as it was conceived as a mass-production exercise enabling more prospective owners to benefit from their 'advanced' designs. Semi-precious stones and enamel were used and sometimes surfaces were covered with hammer marks, in some cases from hand-finishing, and in others to create the illusion of it, the marks being stamped into the metal.

Silver candlestick, height 10 inches, by Waterhouse, Hatfield & Co. of Sheffield, 1843. The decoration has a distinctively Victorian look about it, being elaborate in a heavy sort of way.

Silver

In most fields, the enterprise of colonial American craftsmen was seriously curtailed by the mother country, where Guilds of long standing protected their interests against inroads from the settlers. The Silversmiths' Guild was particularly vigilant, it seems, for one finds all too little American 17th- and 18th-century silver.

There were even proportionately fewer candlesticks made. A native silver source was found in 1858—the Comstock Lode—and only then was silver made in quantity. Even so, cheaper electroplating and other silver substitutes were more widely distributed.

During the late 1800s, styles followed an eclectic assemblage of European designs, continued to this day. Mechanical production had made great strides and classic patterns were turned out in their thousands, in an artistically-frustrating assembly line.

The reaction against this culminated in the Arts and Crafts movement in England and Glasgow, and in Art Nouveau's sinuous, fine curving designs which were difficult to reproduce mechanically. Both these new influences revitalized American design.

The Gorham Manufacturing Co.'s English designer, William Codman, developed a new line of Art silver, hand-made, with typical Art Nouveau swirling plant forms. Their most popular ware of this kind was called Martelé, and many candlesticks and candelabra were produced. Other companies making Art Nouveau included Sterling Co. and Unger Bros.

At the same time, the Arts and Crafts movement, exhibiting in Boston in 1897, inspired Goodnow and Jenks, and their silver showed the same straight, sturdy lines and simple, restrained decoration. Popular all over Europe and America, it led directly to the Scandinavian Modern look of the 1920s, 30s and later.

The simplicity of Arts and Crafts and the natural forms of Art Nouveau both combined in Japanese design. Throughout this period, and again in the 1920s, many pieces reflect this influence.

Silver of this period is still not very expensive, and there were so many styles and patterns from about 1895 onwards that a representative collection could be built up quickly.

Left, pair of American sterling silver candlesticks, height 5 inches, c. 1920, marked with a penguin with a 'g' on its stomach. Their bell-like floral shapes are suggestive of bluebells, probably influenced by the vogue for tasteful Japanese floral shapes popular in the late-Victorian period and onwards. Right, single sterling silver candlestick, American, 1920s, height 8 inches, in the English Georgian style.

Sheffield Plate

The 18th century was a period when the numbers of merchant families were growing and the demand for fine silver was growing with them. Increased competition among silversmiths caused a search for ways to produce silver articles more cheaply. Casting heavy silver gave way to a technique developed in Sheffield which consisted of using thin sheets of stamped metal to make the basic form and then loading the candlestick with resin to give it stability. Another method of providing cheaper candlesticks was to fuse a layer of silver onto copper and then to manufacture the resulting silver-plated sheets into various objects.

Early silver-plated articles came to be known as Old Sheffield Plate, now greatly admired by collectors. The technique, invented by Thomas Boulsover in 1742 and commercialized by Joseph Hancock from about 1758, both of Sheffield, was used to make articles in styles identical to those in solid silver.

The thinness of the silver used for weighted candlesticks and plating varied. The poorer quality ones are likely to have worn through by this century or the last and to have been plated over. This is something the connoisseur will be wary of, for it means that the article is no longer genuinely 18th-century. In the case of Sheffield Plate, it is no bad thing to find the copper showing through, for this indicates that the candlestick has not been replated and thereby renewed to such an extent that the signs of wear and history are gone.

Unlike solid silver, much Sheffield Plate is unmarked. In fact, in 1773 an Act was introduced that forbade the striking of marks on silver-plated items or wares made of silver substitute. In 1784 another Act allowed for the maker's marks, but many makers still did not bother to use them.

This candlestick of Old Sheffield Plate inscribed 'John Hancock Inven.' 1744' with the initials 'JH' over the inscription is a mystery, as the name of the man who invented a method of manufacturing silver-plated candlesticks and other items was Joseph Hancock. However, as he often imposed 'JH' on items by him, possibly 'John' was his other name.

Plated silver 2

One of Sheffield's many claims to fame was the telescopic candle-stick, made in both solid and plated silver. Its appeal was clearly functional. It was adjustable to a height of about $6\frac{1}{2}$ inches to 12 inches, and the light could be varied in this way, according to requirements. Reproductions of these candlesticks were made about the turn of the last century and many reproductions of Old Sheffield Plate have been, and are still, made on plated copper.

The proportion of silver to copper used in plating decreased in the 19th century to allow a greater number of cheaper candlesticks and other plated items to be made, and quality thus deteriorated. From about 1845 a silver-coloured base metal using nickel ('German silver') was used that did not show through the silver as obviously as did copper.

Electro-plating, the process by which silver was deposited on a base metal by electrolysis, was patented in 1840 and soon led to objects being made still more easily and cheaply. This process is used to this day.

As far as style is concerned, plated silver always followed solid silver styles. It is important to be able to recognize that manufacturers sometimes set their plate-marks in little boxes which at a short distance would resemble hall-marks. Presumably this was done in the hope that guests would not know the difference, but it has been known to fool the inexperienced collector. English plate is usually marked EPNS, or with the manufacturer's initials. Solid silver is always hall-marked.

Pair of plated telescopic candlesticks of c. 1830, height extending from $8\frac{1}{2}$ to $10\frac{1}{2}$ inches. These are still much in demand and continue to be made today.

Alabaster

Alabaster is a semi-transparent gypsum resembling marble in appearance though it is much softer in substance. It is finely grained and of a pure white or delicately tinted colour. Some varieties are elegantly veined, striped or spotted. Sometimes alabaster is beautifully banded and is then known as onyx. Great numbers of beautiful ornamental objects such as candlesticks, vases and statuettes have been made of this material, notably in Italy. The designs are almost always classically simple.

In the late 18th century, alabaster was used—as were marble and a softer marble-like mineral known as Blue John or Derbyshire Spar—to make ornamental objects including candlesticks mounted in ormolu. Such items were owned by the wealthy of the period and were a speciality of the famous Birmingham firm of Matthew Boulton.

Oriental alabaster is different and harder than ordinary alabaster. It is really a variety of marble and is found in Egypt where it was worked in ancient times into urns, jars and small containers for oils and perfumes. The latter were known as 'alabastra' (after a town in Egypt) even when not fashioned from alabaster. Hence the derivation of our word.

Western alabaster scratches, and is slightly soluble in water, and should therefore be treated with care.

Alabaster was imitated in glass, but wealthier Americans bought imported pieces and displayed them with pride. Larger candlesticks were sometimes turned into lamps, so that the light reflected the beautiful material.

Italian alabaster candlestick, height 5 inches, c. 1900, made in the naturalistic form of mistletoe and berries, probably designed to sit among holly branches on the dinner- or tea-table or on the mantelpiece during the Christmas season.

Novelties

Those with collecting instincts are very often attracted to the novel in any field. The taste for novelties during Victorian times was nothing new, for certain people had always demanded unusual items with which to amuse themselves and impress their friends.

A collection of novelty candlesticks would largely be confined to this century and the end of the last, for candle-holders were, during most of their history, too vital to everyday existence to be treated lightly, although a collection of early travelling candlesticks, for instance, would be unusual as they are comparatively rare.

In America, where the population leapt from 39,000,000 in 1869 to 100,000,000 in 1915 and to over 200,000,000 today, the number of native collectables available has not equalled demand, an imbalance which has caused Americans to look to the antiques of other countries and very recent bygones from their own.

The animal-foot and animal-horn candlesticks shown here are typical of novelty and souvenir ware that also housed other useful items such as inkwells, pencil-holders, letter-openers and ashtrays. They would be ideal for the hunter's den or study.

Novelty horn and foot candlesticks, each 7 inches high. The horn is mounted on brass and the foot on wood. They are very likely late 19th-century in date, when the taste for novelty combined with the availability of unusual materials like these enabled such individual items to be made.

Plastic

The development of plastics is an interesting field for study and one that is engaging collectors more and more. Plastic candlesticks such as those pictured here are splendid examples from an era when this product, later to become associated with poor-quality goods, was used in expensive furniture and jewellery as an important material in its own right.

As early as 1862, a plastic called Parkesine was invented by Alexandre Parkes. A patent for the famous Bakelite used in the Art Deco period of the 1920s and '30s was taken out by Leo Hendrick Baekeland in 1909. Celluloid, to become so important in the film industry, was also developed around the turn of the century. The word 'plastics' came into current use in England in the 1930s. By the '40s, production was highly sophisticated, particularly in the United States where Plexiglas and Lucite were being developed. Plastic became the fifth class of material after metal, wood, glass and ceramics.

Plastic candlesticks are often stamped with a patent number, enabling one to date them by referring to the patent records. They are less rarely stamped with a maker's name. However, style is usually an immediate clue to dating. Plastic lent itself to the bold geometric shapes typical of much Art Deco.

The pair of white plastic candle-holders, diameter 4 inches, epitomize the stark geometrical shapes, in this case straight lines and circles, prevalent in the 1930s. The orange candlestick, height 7 inches, also made in the 30s, has a neo-classical feel in the fluted column. Its plastic composition is highly resinous and it was meant to have a hard, mottled look rather like tortoiseshell.

Bibliography

BOGER, L. A. and BOGER, H. B. *The Dictionary of Antiques and the Decorative Arts.* New York, 1967 and London, 1969.

BONNIN, A. *Tutenag and Paktong.* Oxford, 1924.

CAMERON, I. and KINGSLEY-ROWE, E. *Encyclopedia of Antiques.* London and Glasgow, 1973.

COMSTOCK, H. (editor). *The Concise Encyclopedia of American Antiques.* New York, 1969.

COYSH, A. W. *Blue-Printed Earthenware 1800-1850.* Newton Abbot, 1972 and Vermont, 1971.

CURLE, A. O. 'Domestic Candlesticks from the Fourteenth to the End of the Eighteenth Century,' *Proceedings of the Society of Antiquaries of Scotland 1925-1926,* Volume LX, 5th Series, Vol 12, pp. 183-214.

FIELD, R. and GENTLE, R. *English Domestic Brass 1680-1810 and the History of its Origins.* London and New York, 1975.

HARRIS, I. *The Price Guide to Antique Silver.* Woodbridge, 1969.

HARRIS, I. *The Price Guide to Victorian Silver.* Woodbridge, 1971.

HILLIER, B. *Art Deco.* London and New York, 1968.

HILLIER, B. *The World of Art Deco.* London and New York, 1971.

HOWE, B. *Antiques from the Victorian Home.* London and New York, 1973.

HUGHES, B. G. *The Country Life Collector's Pocket Book.* London, 1963.

KANOF, A. *Jewish Ceremonial Art and Religious Observance.* New York, 1970.

KLEIN, D. *All Colour Book of Art Deco.* London, 1975.

Liberty's 1875-1975: Catalogue of Exhibition at Victoria and Albert Museum. London, 1975.

MADSEN, S. T. *Art Nouveau.* London and New York, 1967.

MICHAELIS, R. F. *British Pewter.* London, Sydney and New York, 1969.

MORLEY-FLETCHER, H. *Meissen.* London and New York, 1971.

PEAL, C. A. *British Pewter and Britannia Metal for Pleasure and Investment.* London and New York, 1971.

PHILLIPS, P. (editor). *The Collectors' Encyclopedia of Antiques.* London and New York, 1973.

PINTO, E. H. *Treen and Other Wooden Bygones.* London, 1969.

TAIT, H. *Porcelain.* London, New York, Sydney and Toronto, 1966.

VOSE, R. H. *Glass.* London, 1975.

WILLS, G. *Candlesticks.* Newton Abbot, 1974.

YARWOOD, D. *The English Home.* London and Pennsylvania, 1956.

Picture acknowledgements

Page numbers given, those in italics refer to colour.

Christopher Sykes Antiques, Woburn: 13, *27*, 41, *43*, *75*, *89*, 99. The Showcase Antiques, Great Neck, New York: *15*, *35*, 37, 39, 53, *59*, 67, *71*, 73, 81, *83*, 91, *103*. Privately owned: 17, *93*. Cooper Bridgeman Library, London: 19. Josiah Wedgwood and Sons Limited, Stoke-on-Trent: 21. William Bedford Antiques, Islington: *23*, *87*. Dan Klein Antiques, Islington: *25*, 31, *107*. Lee Berman, Little Neck, New York: *29*, *55*, *65*, 97. Twickenham Galleries; Mrs M. Hallam: 33. Author's collection: 45, *51*, 69, 101. William Bedford Antiques, Islington; Author's collection: *47*. The Place off Second Avenue for Antiques, New York: 49, 61. William Bedford Antiques, Islington; Twickenham Galleries: 57. The Meating Place, Port Washington, New York: 63, *77*. Then Antiques, Great Neck, New York: *79*. Then Antiques, Great Neck, New York; Lee Berman, Little Neck, New York: *85*. Sotheby's Belgravia, London: 95. The Place off Second Avenue for Antiques, New York; The Meating Place, Port Washington, New York: 105.

The following photographer's were commissioned to take photographs for this book:
A.C. Cooper Limited, London: 13, 17, *23*, *25*, *27*, 31, 33, 41, *43*, 45, *47*, *51*, 57, 69, *75*, *87*, *89*, *93*, *107*.
Bob Shewchuk Productions, New York: *15*, *29*, *35*, 37, 39, 49, 53, *55*, *59*, 61, 63, *65*, 67, *71*, 73, *77*, *79*, 81, *83*, *85*, 91, 97, *103*, 105.

Index

7509630

STRATTON, D.
3.50

CANDLESTICKS

749.63.

HERTFORDSHIRE LIBRARY SERVICE

This book is due for return on or before the date shown. You may extend its loan by bringing the book to the library or, once only, by post or telephone, quoting the date of return, the letter and number on the date card, if applicable, and the information at the top of this label.

The loan of books in demand cannot be extended.

RENEWAL
INFORM-
ATION

L.32A

CENTRAL STOCKS UNIT
TAMWORTH ROAD
HERTFORD SG13 7DG
TEL: 586 863

10/12

CENTRAL RESOURCES
LIBRARY
0707-281530

11 JUN 1994   16 DEC 1994

1 DEC 1992

21.10.94

10 MAR 1995

2 5 MAR 1995

29 APR 1995

12 JUN 1995

24 JUL 1995
-9 OCT 1995

-3 JAN 1996
10 JAN 1996
1996
-4 APR 1996
30 JAN 1997
26 FEB 1997
16 OCT 1997
1/APR/98
2 6 JAN 2010

L 33